Sex Is Not The Problem, <u>Activation</u> of Lust Is!

Apostle Carolyn Edwards

Printed in the United States of America.

ISBN: 0615609007
ISBN-13: 978-0615609003

Published & Distributed By:
Doors of Life

Cited in this Book
Scripture Quotation Marked Kava Bible Are Taken From The King James Version Bible, Copyright Thomas Nelson Bibles Www. Thomas Nelson.Com 2003 Thomas Nelson Inc.

This Book Is Dedicated To You!

Before you were born, God planned this moment in your life. It is no accident that you are holding this book. God longs for you to discover the life he created for you to live here on earth and in eternity. It is in Christ that we find out who we are and what we are living for. Before we first heard of Christ, he had his eye on us. He had his designs on us for glorious living. This is a part of the overall purpose he is working out in everything and every person life. *Ephesians 1:11*

I am grateful to the hundreds of writers, teachers, spiritual, classical and contemporaries for your support. Thank you to all of those people who have shaped my life and helped teach me these truths. I thank God first, and then my husband Bishop Lyle Edwards, for his love devotion and support. To my daughter Duchess LyAsiah Edwards, who is an inspiration to all who has met her!

I say I love you to my devoted little sister Mildred (Polly) Braswell, and sisters in Christ, Kim Milton & Carmen - thanks for your support. I thank my brothers, Jimmy Brooks & Jeff Rogers. Dr. Apostle Shaunette Houghton thanks to you, for giving me this assignment to teach. Dr. Cathy Rowell I honor you for going to God and making me write the book. I salute the entire family both spiritual and natural for the privilege of sharing these truths with you.

Table of Contents

Introduction

Introduction

Sex is something I thought I knew a lot about, but I have come to realize that my information came from the dark side. I have come into an awareness that God gave us the blue print that we should follow. When it comes to sex I know you are saying "Boring!" Baby you got that thing twisted...

Having Sex the way God has ordained it is better than the 4th of July fireworks! God is explosive. God knows how to fulfill your mind, body and soul to the point you will never look at another God. God gave us our imagination. Most Christians do not know the difference between sex and perversion. The church says sex is wicked. Our teenagers are destroying themselves through the church, due to no one wanting to address their problem.

Pastor Spears use to say in her sermon "My people are destroyed for lack of knowledge **Hosea 4:6**. Most sexual experiences or molestations were by someone we knew or trusted. Therefore our first

3

knowledge of sex was tainted by rape, abuse, rejection, abandonment, etc.

Now I have obtained abandonment issues, rejection, fear and shame. I felt as though I would fall for any person that told me I look good. I was broken. Thinking back over the many years of my life, I found that broken promise took my eyes off my Lord and Savior Jesus Christ. I lost my

focus.

Chapter 1

Virginity (Adam & Eve)

God decided to make man in his own image (Genesis 1:26). The man Adam was born with the female Adam on the inside of him. (Genesis 2:21-23). Virginity is pure and clean. Information obtained by several theologians stated: "That Adam & Eve" were virgins and when the enemy told Eve to look at and eat the forbidden fruit tree (Genesis 3:6). She disobeyed the word of God; the lust was able to enter into her heart. Now we know where the seed of lust came from and how it entered into the blood -line of mankind. What we need to understand is virginity.

Virginity is a state of purity, even though sinful thoughts can come through your mind to make you feel nasty. Having a virgin mind- set will keep you stable in your decision making, and allow you to stay

5

in constant communication with God. The almighty God can talk and download information to you any time he desires. You will receive an overflow of spiritual information. God gave you your heart as a secret place to worship. Virginity is something God gives. God's, people need to be careful who they share their bodies with! It is so easy to develop an ungodly soul tie to a person that God never intended for us to develop a relationship with. Virginity will allow you to have an innocent relationship with your spouse and God. Adam and Eve were virgins in their bodies and minds. Their relationship with God made it impossible for them to think negative thoughts. When the enemy showed up on the scene and put his face where it didn't belong all innocence was lost.

Chapter 2

Lust (David & Bathsheba)

D avid was a man after God's own heart. David was in a season of war at this time of his life. He decided to send his men to war without their leader (2 Samuel 11:1). When God calls you to a war, place you as head of the operation and gives you an assignment, never send someone else in your place! Their relationship with God might not be on the same level as yours. Whosoever God calls, that is who God wants to do the assignment. This does not mean you are better than the next person, it just means you have surrendered all and you are walking in total humility to the almighty God.

David was on his sabbatical. David became restless. The enemy is always waiting on an opportunity to break a covenant relationship with

7

God and his people. David had no business being at home in this season of his life. The enemy, Satan saw the opportunity to set the king up and the devil took it, why did the devil set him up? The devil was able to set David up because he had lost his focus. God was nowhere in the picture. David's discernment did not kick in. This is for all the deep people in Christ you can't give instructions to, because they always say "God already gave it to me!" Come on you know what I mean; those so called prophets that always have a word for you from the lord, you better watch them.

One day the king decided to take a walk on the roof top to get some fresh air. (I promise you baby, don't get it twisted). The day David decided to walk on the roof, Bathsheba was taking a bath. David saw a beautiful lady washing herself (2 Samuel 11:2-4). I smell a set up from the pit of hell.

Oh well, let's move on with this knowledge, God is downloading in us. When the king saw Bathsheba washing herself he started thinking with his lower head. Forgive me, this, is too real for the fake people that have never admitted to having a nasty thought about a man. I want to ask the people of God where was David's Holy Ghost? Oh I am sorry maybe he had not matured that far in God! We always find a way to justify our mess. Well saints, what happened to his discernment? Scripture says: "He that has an ear to hear let him hear." (St. Matthew 11:15) Oh I know we have a lot of sanctified people in this world, where their Holy Ghost will not allow them to read stuff like this.

Let's move on. Can we keep it real? The fact of the matter is David was in full lust mode, and he saw something he wanted. The king inquired about Bathsheba. David learned she was married. The time of her purification was over. (2 Samuel 11:3) David's lower head was now in full control making all of the decisions from this moment on. David didn't care. He had committed the uttermost sin, lusting after another man's wife. He is the king. "All hail the King!" I beg to differ!

9

God is the head; God is in control of this universe. My Pastor told me once you see something, it is in your mind, but once it goes in your heart, you have done that thing. Repentance is in order if you want to receive your covenant agreement back with God.

When we are in a certain position people over you will want you to compromise you're anointing. These are family curses and they will hunt you until you die. Lust will destroy every relationship you will ever encounter. You will never find a sense of commitment in having a good marriage, when lust is in control. The problem comes when lust has taken control.   Lies will catch up with you. You will realize you have just lost the best gift of your life, trust, when lust takes control. God might not give you the chance to break another woman's heart.

Chapter 3

Activated Lust

Activated lust starts in the mind. A seed is planted from something that grabbed your attention. The seed began to sprout and take root and the root began to grow. Thoughts began to fester on wanting things that do not belong to you. Knowing that it is wrong and out of order, a root has   formed in your mind. Lust has festered through the body.

Now, you begin to have the wet dreams that you have not experienced in the last five years of your marriage. You will begin to pay more attention to the females, at church, work, in the stores and your job to a point that it has consumed your way of thinking. Your decision-making is not stable due to your fantasizing about flesh. All these negative thoughts started in your mind. The key to eliminating lust is staying grounded and rooted in the word of God. Lust will lead you down a path of destruction and before you even realize it has occurred you have lost your entire family, job and friends.

You have worked so hard that everything God has blessed you with is gone. Realizing that this was a trap set to destroy your destiny. Lust will alter your DNA, and you will be right back in the place like David in Psalms 51 when he asked God to wash him clean and white as snow. But this is the key "Boo": If you don't even realize that you have been on a roller coaster ride and you have allowed your flesh to take charge in this matter then Baby, you've got that thang twisted.

The lust spirit is so convincing. Lust will make you think that you have received the deliverance when you were on the altar asking God to forgive you for sleeping with the pastor. You turn around and look at your wife and kids, wondering how to handle the truth if it ever got out that a spirit attacked me and I gave into it. One day while in the pastor's office we were having a meeting. In the middle of the meeting I felt an arousal I realized what happened; I had connected to a part of me that had been hidden for so many years. Something was activated inside of me. Before I could even get a grasp of what was happening; I tried to understand my feelings. I was in full lust mode and the spirit came from the pastor. If you look at me, I look straight as any other man does if you don't have an insight you will never be able to see what had me in bondage.

At this point in my life, I wanted a deliverance from this lust demon. Even when I say no and I am not going to do it again, I find myself right back in that place. My soul is being pulled towards this spirit of lust. I know that it is not right. The spirit of lust was on the pastor. It had activated a lust spirit on the men in his congregation. Other Christian men that the pastor associated himself with are warring unaware with a spirit and only the strong shall survive.

I counseled a woman of God that was part of a mega ministry. She went to her bishop and apostle to ask if she could marry one of the pastor's in their association. They gave her permission to marry the pastor. The day of their wedding, they went back to their apartment. When they went through the door he went to his bedroom. She turned around to see why he was not coming to her bed. Her husband informed her by saying "I'm gay and I needed you to marry me so I would not lose my position in the church conference."

The new bride had been saving herself for her husband for the past 10 years. He activated a lust mode that was lying dormant in her very soul. She fell for the first pair of pants that asked her to be his wife only to find out she had got set up by the "okie-doke." Now, she is a bitter Assistant Pastor wondering why didn't the man or woman of God that was over her soul see the homosexuality spirit in her husband. Why did they give her permission to marry him? How did they overlook his homosexuality? No one could see it because his or her eyes were full of lust. So with that, where was the discernment in the body of Christ? Who was interceding on the woman of Gods behalf?

14

Where were the intercessors? Do they even tap into the spirit realm anymore?

Everybody is caught up in corporate America and overlooking the souls that are being caught up in the enemy's trap. They are crying out for help and they feel like no one is living holy anymore and everybody's soul is on the way to hell. The truth of the matter is "God still has more souls than the devil." (2 Kings 6:16-17) Gahazi said "Alas, my master, how shall we do? He answered, fear not: for they that be with us are more than they that be with them. And Elisha prayed, and said Lord; I pray thee, open his eyes that he may see. And the Lord opened the eyes of the young man; and he saw: and behold, the mountain was full of horses and chariots of fire round about Elisha." They were ready to fight on their behalf. (Don't get it twisted baby, to God be the glory). God sent his angels to fight the enemy and stand in the gap for our lives. So whatever the enemy tells you that you're not going to do, tell him he is a lie.

Activated lust is lust that began when someone touches a person inappropriately, such as a child molester. When you are a little child you have no idea what sex is; suddenly somebody comes along and they begin to tamper with different sensitive areas of our bodies that God has given us, such as our virginity, our innocence and our virgin mind set. Nothing has been able to change what God has given us. Psalm 51 says: "We were born in sin, shaped in iniquity." We came here knowing how to lie, steal and put each other down. Once you have been washed in the blood of the lamb (God) lust is no longer in the picture and you are made whole. When you are dealing with activated lust there is something that someone has downloaded in you that you did not ask for.

I remember when I was a little girl and I began to be molested. I went through the process of trying to understand what was going on within my little body. I was around 6 or 7 years of age when I was molested. I remember being touched improperly and feeling the little sparks and hot waves that were going on within my little body. I felt a feeling in my body I had never experienced. I was experiencing something new in my body. I did not know it was called arousal. A predator older than I called lust was awakening my flesh to sin. I didn't know it was wrong. I flowed with the out of control emotion.

Molestation has been done to many children. What we should know is that a person that is molested will sometimes becomes a molester when they grow up. Society will say they need counseling when they are molested. The Church will say those that have been molested need counseling and deliverance, if they want to be set free from molestation.

Sometimes we think new experiences are good; but some experiences are created to destroy our assignment and our destination. God being so awesome will reroute our destination in life If we stop trying to help God out we would not go through so much in life.

My Pastor preached a sermon one Sunday stating: "trials come to make us strong."

Chapter 4

Activated Lust From Parent

When your parent has an addiction and a mental problem, most of the time they have been abused. A close friend or family member has done this abuse. What happens when your parent thinks there issue is hidden and everybody sees their problem, the spirit inside you is bringing up your past history, which activates the lust demon. Many times you find yourself walking in the street late at night trying to turn a trick. When feeling rejected by your mother or father you will start thinking on how to get even with them due to the feeling of hurt inside. When a mother or father has abused you, you feel they love their mate more than they love you. This is when the lusting spirit starts and you will go after the other person to get the attention from the parent

19

that you feel has rejected your very existence. You will do whatever it take to break them up.

What you have to understand is we are dealing with a demonic spirit that desires to destroy the whole family. Have you ever met a woman that sold her daughters? Many girls sell their little bodies for their drug habit and have no remorse. She will find somebody to blame for her actions, because she can't get over her past and her mother was mean and uncaring towards her. In other words there is a generational curse on the women in this family. Most abused and broken parents learn how to give up on their children and their children's dreams due to the parent never having anyone to support their dreams.

The only job most of these women had from their past was cleaning someone's house, waiting on tables, babysitting someone's children, and settling for a dead beat man that can only please their flesh for five or ten minutes. The only relief they can ever obtain is through Christ Jesus. Once they accept Christ's healing they will be made whole. Then new values, principals and goals can be set for their new life in Christ. When they are ready to come out of living in the gutter, Christ makes them a new creature in him.

Many females that are broken have accepted their fate. The enemy made them think that life would never change for them. Satan will bring along somebody that will treat you like royalty for the first three months. Satan will lure you into thinking that they love you with all of their heart, mind, body and soul. You don't want to see the red flags that stand for warning signs. The man looks at your child more affectionately than he looks at you. Now the man talks up under your clothes and makes negative remarks to you. Your body isn't shaped right! You can't think quickly enough! Your food isn't good any more. Those night conversations and laughter have ceased. And now, he is lusting after your baby girl.

Instead of you covering your daughter you blame her for stealing your man. In actuality, he has torn down your self-esteem and you are in a fighting mode. Instead of fighting the person who caused the problem you will take it out on an innocent child that needs your protection. You want to keep a man no matter what the consequences might be. You will sell your child out to stay with a "nothing Boo." You are out of order!

First thing you need to do is repent and fall back in love with yourself. Ask yourself why you keep allowing people to hurt you? Why do you feel the need to keep allowing people to hurt you and break you down? You are not a garbage can. You are somebody's baby. And even if your parents did not give you the affection that you need, God will always place a servant in your midst to see you through. It's up to you what you do with the blessing that God has sent your way in this season of your life. You need to surround yourself with Godly women.

Don't get it twisted –don't get advice from messy women. Women that always give you free advice are trouble. These people always want to know what's going on in your house. Many of them just want to know how messed up you are. You need someone who is going to encourage you when you don't have a dime to give them; feed you and your children. You need a friend who can call anytime and will pray with you. They won't try to use you or possess you. They just want to try to help you make it to your next level in God.

So hold your head up. You are next in line for a miracle! Don't let the lust spirit make decisions for your life anymore. Stay focused. Take baby steps. One day at a time. And stay grounded and rooted in the word of God because the Word is marrow to the bone. Amen.

"Once they accept Christ's healing they will be made whole."

Chapter 5

Activated Lust in the Body of Christ

To all the First Lady's and Pastor's wives that are struggling with affection issues from the man of God that he made for you. Reality check, lust can easily slip into your very soul. The fact of the matter is your husband's first priority is to the people in the ministry. He is trying to grow spiritually. Sports, and other activates are not important anymore. Friends are no longer his boys because he is now a Christian. His vocabulary has changed. Don't forget, how they talk to you and mistreated, you when no one else was around. They don't want their behavior to appear like something is still left on them from the street. Women of God, let us go back to the threshing floor. We must pray constantly for our men and children. When we have a void in our heart, we will find a substitute to fill that void. We start placing things, people, issues or other people's problems in that spot, or whatever we can find to stop that ache inside our heart.

To the man of God, I know a lot of sanctified women in ministry who have bad attitudes in the body of Christ. Those women have run a lot of people away from the church; God gave her to you to love the hurt away. You will need to have patience toward the women of God. Stop making her feel your attitude every time you talk to her. The enemy is saying look at the division I have caused between the man and woman of the highest God. Your wife can feel when you give another woman more attention than you give her. Neglect will cause your wife to mistreat and talk rude to the women you are extra nice to in the ministry, (1 John1: 7-9) but if we walk in the light, as he is in the light, we have fellowship one with another.

The blood of Jesus Christ cleanses us from all sin. "If we say we have no sin, we deceive ourselves, and the truth is not in us. If we confess our sin, He is faithful and just to forgive us our sin, and to cleanse us from all unrighteousness." This is good for our soul. Please people of God remember the devil has gifts and power. There are lots of people that love God but they don't have any Holy Ghost keeping power; and their blood is still tarnished with sin. According to Romans 10:9-10, "that if thou shall confess with thy mouth the lord Jesus, and shall believe in thine heart that God has raised him from the dead, thou shalt be saved. For with the heart man believeth unto righteousness; and with the mouth confession is made unto salvation."

The Preachers get hit first when they preach the word of God and witness to the world. Who does the preacher go to for counseling when he has problems? When the preacher's life is falling apart, they feel like God has forgotten about them. The enemy will try to bring someone or something back in your present with a lust spirit. This spirit will pull you back into a life full of sin. Baby, you better know that

27

God has saved you for real. Sin is easy to get into, but hard to get out of once you fall. You need to go through a restoration plan to that will lift you back up in Christ. I know the saved people go to God. Sometimes we need to know if another Christian has been through what we are going through; so I will know if I am on the right road to glory. Lust will draw spirits back your way, due to the big gap in your soul. The Devil desires to fill you up with rage, so you will not have any remorse about the way you are acting in public. My problem is I don't want to make God ashamed or look bad. I am delivered from the lust spirit at this time in my life.

God gave me an ex- G to marry from the street. My new husband brought me back to reality about life. I have been raped, molested, beaten, and have had the spirit of witchcraft put on me and in my food. My ex-husband and his mother practiced witchcraft on me. For the people that don't believe, (1 Samuel 28:7-14) talks about the witch at Endor that had a familiar spirit, once you read these scriptures they will tell you that king Saul had gotten rid of all the people in that land that had a familiar spirit and practiced being wizards. Then Acts 8:9-11 talks about a man named Simon who used sorcery and bewitched the people in that city. He bewitched them for a long time. The people believed he was the real thing.

Witchcraft is going on in the body of Christ today. If you do not have members in your church people will consider you as a nobody but Boo, you got that thing twisted... God will visit every church unless you don't want him in your house.

My Ex-husband had a lust demon in him. He would pin me down and abuse me until he got tired. Don't judge me if you don't know my story. You will never understand my glory in God. I am free today to worship. Take whatever you need to glean from this book to be set free or release from bondage in this time of your life. I have experienced being awakened in my flesh by a man of God.

You must understand I have been delivered from my lust demon in my flesh for the last 10 years of my life. The spirit of lust tried to mess me up. To have a man of God eyes make contact with my private body parts as if it was his little secret lust. His lust spirit made me feel degraded. We need to be careful. You don't know who in your presence might have an insight and can see or hear you through the spirit realm.

The problem is I was nowhere in that vicinity, and I got pulled into his mess. This attraction made me feel like I was back in the streets turning tricks. (*Please don't get it twisted*) I was not born in the church, I grew up in the church and my mother was the pastor of the church back in Birmingham, Alabama. So what?! I am country plus old school. I was raised by them old saints that use to flow in the spirit in the sanctuary every Sunday morning. The spirit of the lord was in that little building. I thank God for my roots. I thank God for my spiritual insight; it let me know how and where to pray, for my own self.

Back to the man of God, he was in full lust mode. A person that is walking in the spirit where you have been delivered from can see the residue of the spirit that used to be. The first thing that is going to take place is the lusting spirit is trying to bring you out of retirement. The man of God's wife had put him on strike, that means no sex at all. *Boo you are out of order!* 1 Corinthians 11:8-11 "for the man is not of the woman but the woman of the man neither was the man created for the woman: but the woman for the man". What I am trying to say is your body is not yours, it belongs to your husband and his body belongs to you so stop bargaining with your tail/behind (whatever your pet name is for your body parts!)

Please don't get deep on me now! Can we keep it real? One day you are going to wake up and find out another tail has taking your place. If you don't take care of home it will take care of itself.

The enemies job is to separate the husband and wife so their ministry will die. This man loves God but the spirit of lust had taken over his holy ghost, I don't care how deep you are in God or what your title is, the devil will find any roots or stones that are left in your heart and he will expose you to the fullest. Never think your secret is safe with the enemy. Sometimes your secret isn't even safe with the church folk.

Chapter 6

Activated Lust in Teenagers

Today, teenagers are caught between a rock and a hard place. They will fall for any lie that the devil throws at them. Most children just want to fit in somebody's circle. The outbreak of homosexuality is due to a lot of kids trying to fit into a circle - they feel like the church has rejected them and thrown them out on the streets. The parents are so embarrassed that their child is having relations with the same sex, they stop praying for their children. The parents seem to have turned their backs on them. This is not the way God wanted us to embrace our children.

Stop getting caught up in the negativity and get stronger in your prayer life. We can intercede for our nation of children - straight, bisexual, or crooked. All they see is a lot of phony people in the body of Christ.

Many believe having a relationship with the same sex is right. Oh well! I have ministered to so many teenagers about their parents. The children are tired of being fussed at, cussed at and told what to do. There is no one to hug the children; Private time is not spent with the children we have birthed these babies in a chaotic world. The world is full of destruction and our prayer life is not up to par so we are not covering our children. We are not being covered also. People of God please maintain a prayer life so the spirit of the living God can dwell within your arena.

When a teenager is walking a straight path, and they run into a child that is bisexual and trying to do their own thing, our teenagers discernment is not in a position to be able to warn them against the danger of what's about to take place in their little lives. Before they realize it, they are in the sack with a bisexual person teaching them about their sexuality not even realizing the person they are in the bed with has no idea about their own sexuality. And, most of all, teenagers go along with it because they don't feel loved, they want their heads to be bashed because they are trying to prepare themselves to come home and deal with us (parents).

I was told by a teenager that the parents are warring with the streets .The streets are winning because when they hang out with other teenagers, they don't argue with each other, they don't make them clean up the house, they don't tell them to go to bed, they don't tell them to cook. They don't have to worry about hearing the mouths of their parents fussing. He said, "We only see and hear our parents three times a day." Their parents always say get up, clean up your room, and then go to bed. Many parents never show affection or give hug or kisses to their children. This is why rejection has set in the children hearts. Now their attitude is "I don't give a damn" - and that's for the deep people that are so sanctified. This is one of the reasons why many children unite and fight against their parents not realizing that the lust spirit has been activated within their very souls. They just feel more loyal to the children than they do to the parents and the parents are still saying, "I don't get it". You need to go on a fast and ask God for direction.

We need to understand that when a straight person hangs out with a gay person those spirits will hop on the weaker vessel. I have ministered to many of young people that say "They accept me for who I am. I felt good about myself for the first time in my life." A lot of people say they are too young to know what love is. I beg the difference; most of our babies know about sex as they reach 12 years of age. Many have been raped, beaten, sold for drugs, or have no food to eat. Once the lust spirit takes hold on them, God help their little soul. A lot of them know it is wrong because they were reared in the church. My husband and I started our first church in Brooklyn; NY. The church was full of ex-homosexual, gay women, prostitutes and homeless people. Most homosexuals never went to church to become a born again Christian.

My husband and I had street revival and tent meetings in the projects. We had no plans to start a church. God always sent the people to us! And one thing is for sure if you don't want God for real you will not be able to stay in a real old school church. The broken and abused child with issues grow up to be a parent with problems that were never dealt with. The parent begins to have children out of wedlock, that means they weren't married. We wonder why our children are born with lustful spirits, ADHD, behavioral disorders, and mental problems. The reason for this is most of the woman have more than one man in their life. Each time they lay with one of them the spirit on the man transfers to the baby. (I am just the mail lady! I deliver the mail, I don't write it).

If you have been engaged with someone over several years you need to rethink about that marriage. I know money is a factor when you are planning a wedding. The courthouse is not that far from you. You are saying "Lord Help me with this spouse." You want your children to understand he or she has a problem and God told you to help them. The children see him coming out of your bedroom. He is not your husband. You want to whip the children when they go and have sex. The children are only doing what they see the parents do. (You got that thing twisted, I promise you baby).

When you allow a spirit to roam freely in your house the lust spirit will get on everything that is not covered by the blood of God. Boo, let me tell you something you can't compromise your anointing and think it will still work. (Romans 1:24-28) "Wherefore God gave them up to uncleanness through the lust of their own hearts, to dishonor their own bodies between themselves: Who changed the truth of God into a lie, and worshipped and served the creature more than the creator, who is blessed forever Amen. For this cause God gave them up into vile affections: for even their woman did change the natural use against that which is against nature: And likewise also the man, leaving the natural use of the woman, burned in their lust one toward another; men with men working that which is unseemly, and receiving in them self that recompense of their error which was meet. And even as they did not like to retain God in their knowledge, God gave them over to a reprobate mind, to do those things which are not convenient."

Please remember the enemy will tell you it's all right to have sex with your mate. You felt he was sent from heaven. If he looks that good to you lust will come and try to pull you into a state of thinking it's alright; because we will be married soon. What if he falls in love with another person and leaves you behind? Now, you want to blame God for your actions. I am not a party pooper but God will not bless any mess.

Most young ladies lock themselves up in the house until their husband comes along to meet them. Due to the fact they still have some lust issues within themselves that they have not been delivered from. On the first date they are afraid of having sex and not being able to hold out for God. If he is still saying he loves you and has not married you, and it has been five long years, something is wrong boo. Don't get it twisted my cousin said to me "Why buy the whole cow when the milk is free?!" Some young men say the best "stuff" is in the church. It's hot, ready and you don't have to pay anything for it.

Some of the teenage children are very disrespectful to their parents. Now, you want to get an attitude. If the shoe fits wear it. Let us pray for the ones that have a lusting problem in the body of Christ. You need to get over the shock because they could be talking about your child. Most homes don't have a positive role model. Most fathers and mothers in this society are hooked up, on drugs, or have some kind of addiction.

Chapter 7

Activated Lust & Loneliness

L oneliness is a place where everybody's path has crossed in his or her life! Lust is a driven spirit that continues to play a rerun in people's lives. When you look at the people of this world, in their diverse mentality, loneliness has hit them all. It has taken them to a place of no return!

For instance, let's look at the pastor of this Church; his wife had died after forty years of marriage. He had been a faithful servant to the lord. He is beginning to get lonely at night. The emptiness that he is feeling from the loss of his wife has brought upon him the spirit of lust. Now he is beginning to let that spirit control his emotions, being the pastor who is the head of the church, the spirit of lust is now affecting his relationship with the sheep in his ministry. With that being said he begins to make love with the females in the congregation with his lustful eyes, he has made contact with one of the sheep that was a loyal assistant to his belated wife. She felt like it was her duty to serve the man of God until no end! She felt as if it was her call and purpose to pick up what her first lady left behind! She does not realize that she has been set up from the pit of hell!

The woman of God prayed to her God about her affair with the pastor. She does not realize that the lonely spirit that became lust in his eyesight has set her up. Now, the spirit of lust has been activated within the woman of God. Her discernment has not picked up Satan's device in deceiving her into thinking she was doing the right thing. The woman of God is still in mourning after her first lady. Her sense of loyalty to the first lady has been distorted she doesn't know where the cut off line is. She feels like she is doing the pastor a huge favor by having a relationship with him.

The pastor is requiring more of her time but he does not want to marry her because it will affect his social security money. If the other church ladies knew the pastor was sleeping with one of the sheep in his body of Christ, he would lose a lot of members. Most of them desired the Pastor for themselves; thinking the he was supposed to be theirs. My problem is where are the prophets in this Church? Never allow the enemy to make you compromise your Holy Ghost.

If you cannot hear from God yourself, seek council from a man or woman of God that you know is living and walking in the way of holiness. You can see the fruit from their labor. This leader now carries the blood on his hands from the souls that he has led astray. Don't get an attitude with me. I'm just the mail lady delivering a message.

The woman of God has a call on her life to serve in ministry. The woman's problem is she is fornicating with the pastor and he doesn't want to marry her. How can she minister to another sister in the ministry with the same issues? Boo you out of order! Don't allow the faces in the ministry to keep you from receiving a full deliverance. If you want to be set free, repent of your actions and be Godly. Go to the altar and leave everything that you are emotionally attached to. Repent from your sins to God. Go before the congregation and ask for forgiveness. After giving your confession go through a restoration period. Then, you can properly be restored back to your position in the body of Christ.

Chapter 8

Loneliness in Women

Loneliness has touched women that have been abused sexually and physically, divorced, broken, rejected and insecure. Many have succeeded in life. Loneliness has made these women fall for men that have no values, principles, or self worth. Loneliness has also made these women stay with a man for the sake of having somebody. These men peep the women's game and know they are not going anywhere because of their low self-esteem. They don't believe that God has someone better for them. He would love and cherish them and promote healing and wholeness in their lives.

Genesis 16: 1 says "Sarah, Abraham's wife got angry with God, because she had no children." She felt like God had restrained her from bearing children.

She got pissed off with God and decided to do her own thang! When you allow the enemy to tap into your mindset and make decisions for you, you will find yourself doing some dumb stuff. Sarah made a decision to let her man go into her handmaiden Hagar. Boo, she's out of order - this is something she didn't realize was going to cut her deep in her heart. She gave her husband to her maid. We wonder why so many housekeepers become the woman and move the wife out of the picture. The wife starts tripping out and accusing her husband of being out of control. In reality she was the blame for the problem that took Abraham to have sex with Hagar. Don't get it twisted. Stop nagging the man about issues within yourself that you don't want to face or deal with. So you find the next flunky that you can have an argument with. This is only to make you feel better within yourself. This is not your fault!

Abraham was a man of God, but one day his wife told him to go have sex with her maid. Abraham was a man of around 100 years of age. In your mind you are going to say my wife is 90 and the maid is around 25 years of age. It was not even a second thought. Abraham lust was activated with his wife's permission and all his equipment stood at attention! Never say what you can't do because if this man could stand at 100, God can do all things. I know it's a lot of sanctified people whose Holy Ghost will not allow them to read stuff like this (I promise you baby, you got that thing twisted).

Hagar was betrayed by her mistress, Sarah. Hagar a young woman saving herself for the newfound God that she saw in the woman of God Sarah. Sarai never asked Hagar would she have sex with her man. She never even considered how Hagar felt about it. Sarai had her own motive and the enemy saw an opportunity and took it. Smells like a setup from the pit of hell.

Anyway, Hagar bared him a son named Ishmael and Sarah became jealous. The fact was that she had no children and the maid did. Now the spirit of loneliness tormented the woman of God, to the point of no return. Hagar despised Sarai for what she made her do and the Lord judged Sarah for her actions. Abraham wanted no part of this quarrel between the two women. In other words, he hit that thang and left. Abraham washed his hands of the whole matter. He left Sarah to deal with the shame of her actions. She felt like God did not keep his promise.

Brokenness made her make a quick fix decision that will haunt her for the rest of her life. She rejected the prophecy that the two men sent from God. God told Abraham that Sarah shall conceive and have a baby but Sarah laughed and said "Will God allow me to be with my husband intimately when my womb has closed up?" What she took for a joke was in fact reality.

If God has given you a word that doesn't even seem real to your own mind, get in the spirit and let the Lord minister to you. This was after God told Sarah she was going to have the promise seed of Abraham. Please people of God, stand on the promised word of God. Don't allow loneliness to make decisions for your life that you can never change.

"If God has given you a word that doesn't even seem real to your own mind, get in the spirit and let the Lord minister to you."

Chapter 9

Activated Lust in Toddlers

P arents should be aware that there is such a thing as activated lust in toddlers. They learn by what they see and not what you say, but what you say and how you say it is important. As parents, we need to be careful of the things we do and say around our children. Children will mimic you and what you say. This will affect their character. They will act out of character if you act out of **character**.

Children will fight if you continually hit them. They are not old enough to understand "stop." Stop has more than one meaning; you have used it repeatedly for everything. We have to find words to convey the desired behavior, which will facilitate their vocabulary as well.

Children are trying to find their identity, space

and how much they can get away with. How much you will allow before you give up? Stay focused! You are your Childs 1st role model. Don't get it twisted; we need to be aware of how we give them a bath. This may cause an awakening of sensitive areas too soon. The areas we are washing are sensitive and we need to pray before we bathe them. Dormant spirits of lust in us can and will transfer to our children causing them to act out.

Boo, I know you are saved and I know you loving on God. You can still have some roots to trees that were chopped down years ago. Paul said we are to die daily. In our mind we think that we are so sanctified. A lot of us are just satisfied with no anointing. Our children get left behind by some parents, school and other authority figures. What they learn they get it from the streets. The enemy is waiting for the opportunity to bring all things negative in their lives. We always want to help someone else rear their children when your own children are tore up from the floor up!

Satan will taken advantage of our children. Specifically when there is a call on the child's life Satan will attack. We need to guard their sexuality with all diligence. The spirit of homosexuality is lurking looking for an empty vessel. In this society the children feel there is nothing wrong with same sex relationships. They are loyal to their friends, instead of the parents. Parents feel that they didn't rear their child in a negative way. The role of those spirits is to alter the child's destination in God.

We need to be aware of our surroundings. When dressing children and toilet training we must be careful. We are to make them aware that certain things are private acts and are not shared with anyone outside of their caregivers. Diaper changing needs to be guarded. Parents should be aware that lust could be activated even at this sensitive age.

My 3 year old loves to look at her nakedness in the mirror. She has located her pocket book (vagina) and to her that is the best thing she has found in her little world. I need you to understand that this thing messed me up. After talking to her about her little body she still plays with it. She is fascinated by her body. After much talking, fasting, praying, and laying it at the altar my 3-year still explores her body.

We must understand that this will be a topic of much repetition. Until they can judge for themselves please do not give up on your child. We always want to protect our seed from the enemy. We must be aware that the enemy has already got a hit out on their anointing. He knows that the call on his or her life is great. They will be a prophet to the nations. If the enemy can stop him or her before they ever become of age, he won't have to worry about the souls the children will bring into the kingdom of God.

Spirits will attach themselves to the children born to holy parents. Parents who are walking with God and walking in oneness with God produce a holy seed. The enemy uses any door to enter and wreak havoc in the life of the child. People of God please stay focused on the assignment of God for your child. Please pray for all of the children attached to you. They will influence your seed. There is a predator on every side waiting to devour our children. Don't get it twisted baby, your status in God does not make you immune to the devices of your enemies. You have been given weapons to wage effective warfare on behalf of your seed so they will fulfill their destiny.

"…your status in God does not make you immune to the devices of your enemies."

Chapter 10

Conclusion

A lot of people wonder why they have problems with lust. You need to know where you come from. For instance; my grandfather's father was a stud. In slavery times a man would be used to make women pregnant. The women on the plantation had babies so they could have more help in the cotton field. I learned that my great grandfather had two other women living with him in his house, besides his wife and they were all pregnant at the same time. Oh my God, look at the generational curse on the men in my family.

I am not saying that every man in my family has this problem but a lot of them do, don't get it twisted. These men don't realize they need to go through deliverance to be set free. Not just going through the motion of attending church. Due to a lust spirit that has been placed on them from their forefathers they experience rejection. They feel like they must have more than one woman at a time.

Many homes have been destroyed due to men thinking they needed a spare tire (woman) or trying to fill up the notches on their belt. You need to know the sign of a generational curse. In the bible (2 king 5:25-27) Gehazi and his descendant was cursed with leprosy due to a lie. We tell our children to be better than us. The truth is we are our children's first role model. You can talk until you are blue in the face. So, the truth of the matter is whatever spirit you are housing, the same thing will come up in your seed. You may feel like your family may be better off without you but you are wrong. Every child needs to know where they come from so the family curse can be nipped in the bud.

My son informed me throughout the experience of his life with his father that he would never name his son after him due to the family curses. Alcohol, drugs, abandonment and rejection are all spirits. I am proud of his success in life. He has had his share of problems in his life but he made it through and so can you. I've learned you can do all things through Christ Jesus who gives us strength in knowing, that the darkest night is just before day break.

Don't subject yourself to being a victim of the enemy plans for your life. Activated lust will destroy your destiny. Know you are more than a conquerer under the authority of the Holy Spirit. Possess power on a super-natural – level, in a natural world. The only way to receive success from any issues you may be dealing with from this book is, YOU MUST HAVE A RELATIONSHIP WITH GOD.

As I have experienced many things throughout my life that have caused me pain, anger, heart break, and longsuffering, yet, through my personal relationship with God, He saw fit to heal, deliver and set my captured soul free. I received a new found love, joy and refreshing of my mind, body, and soul.

More importantly this is much more than lusting for random sex or having a long term sexual relationship. This will lead you to lusting after somebody else that does not belong to you. Now, I don't claim to be a Super-Woman, and yes there will be some rough times, and some lonely nights here or there, but our God is awesome!!

Through your personal relationship you will find that there is no other love like God. Only after you experience real love with him will you truly   be able to give and receive love. Love will stand against the test of time, throughout your life-span and remain everlasting. We are indebted to God the author and finisher of our faith.

Chapter 11

Steps to Prevention

After deliverance takes place the lust spirit will try to pierce your soul.

1. Worship -- When you bow down on your knees put your head between your legs and cry out to God. That is a form of intimacy when you are exalting God. Worship is also becoming one with your creator, allowing him to be the lover of your soul so the enemy won't make you feel ashamed.

2. Rebuke -- Thoughts that play in your mind like a rerun, what and how you use to do your sexual business, Turn off the TV in your head. Those moving pictures are dangerous. They will lead you to lusting after something you can't have which will lead you to sin.

3. Prayer -- Keeps you away from those ungodly relationships that have developed an ungodly soul

tie. Lord Help! I can't date because I'm afraid I might give up some tail.

4. Word -- When the lust of the streets is calling you from within; stay at home and study God's word.

5. Deliverance -- Will prevent you from cheating on your spouse and keep you from beating your head up against the wall every time you fall short. Scripture says there is therefore now no condemnation to those who are in Christ.

About the Author

Apostle Carolyn Edwards was spiritually educated under the leadership of her mother Pastor Mary Lee Spears. She was trained and taught the way of Holiness. Before going into ministry, Apostle Carolyn worked with dysfunctional families in the state of Alabama for 7 years as a family care Specialist, Counselor and Mentor. After a life of physical and mental abuse, depression, anxiety, molestations, rapes, divorces and many more trials and tribulation, she accepted the call of God on her life. Carolyn served as a faithful disciple and after the passing of her mother Pastor Spears, she was ordained the Pastor of Faithful Few International Church.

As time passed Carolyn began to travel from state to state and internationally. God called her to Lansing, Michigan where she founded a ministry for hurting woman called Woman of Pain. Her journey continued on to Chicago, Illinois. Carolyn met and married

Bishop Lyle Edwards. They began to travel around the country teaching, preaching, equipping, establishing and overseeing churches. Currently, Carolyn and her husband are overseers of several churches throughout the United States.

Apostle Edwards is a strong believer of the word of God and walks what she talks. She preaches the uncompromising, hard-core doctrine. She walks in the office of Prophet. The anointing that flows from her is like a two-edge sword.

Currently Apostle Edwards is the founder and Sr. Pastor along with her husband Bishop Lyle Edwards of The True Anointing Deliverance Ministry International Inc. Their church is located at 2819 West 71st street, Chicago, IL 60629.